Rough Roads

Rafik Romdhani

Published by
Wheelsong Books
4 Willow Close,
Plymouth PL3 6EY,
United Kingdom

Print ISBN 979-8-84959-417-0

I would like to dedicate Rough Roads (my third collection of poetry) to the soul of my grandmother, Fatma Jbili, the best grandmother anyone could ever hope for.

She used to encourage me to dream big and follow my dreams till they came to fruition. I can remember her murmuring mind-blowing songs during her darkest and bluest hours which I think are still inspiring today.

She always offered comfort when the outside world showed itself to be heedless and indifferent, and gave me incredible adage. She was a woman of wisdom and deep thoughts even though she never attended a school.

Thank you grandmother, for everything you gave.

May your soul rest in peace forever.

Contents

Foreword

Rafik Romdhani is an extraordinary poet. His first collection for Wheelsong Books, titled *Dance of the Metaphors (2021)*, was a book filled with his imagination, brimming over with invention and suffused with magical wordplay and imagery. *Rough Roads* is the second collection published by Wheelsong Books, and if anything, it is an even stronger and bolder statement of Rafik's prowess as both a wordsmith and imagineer.

His work is infused with North African life and marinated in Arabic culture. It resounds with the rich sounds and flavours of his life experiences. You may sense an element of discomfort, but also a scent of the familiar, as you read Rafik's poetry. The words will jar you and comfort you in equal measure, and that is the subtle art of this poet. He will draw you in, shake you up and slowly let you settle into a realisation that possibly, this poem might just be about you...

Steve Wheeler, FRSA
Plymouth, England
September 2022

Preface

Poetry is a window into introspective thoughts. It is a genuinely wide open window onto art in itself, where the unthinkable and the weird can occur to make things happen by the power of words. Poetry exposes the invisible nooks deep inside us to create an ample space of the metaphysical, through metaphorical propensities and mysteries. Poetry instructs language what to do and causes words to discover a new meaning. It is an artform that recreates reality and a way of beading words into worlds that paint and elucidate the possible versions of ourselves that the future might hold.

Rough Roads is my third poetry collection following on from *Dance of the Metaphors* and *The Crash of Verses*. It moves beyond the mere chronicling of events throughout the life of the bard to become a deep reflection upon the self against the boundless depths of existence. It is both a vision and a re-vision of skin-to-skin realities; an ongoing exploration of metaphors, and much more.

In this collection, words seem to brush against each other and even crash together to explode, forging the path that takes the reader to the great beyond – and deeply inward as well – In this collection I find myself rethinking and rearranging poeticized recollections under a rainbow of labyrinthine complex ruminations – where a new being struggles to be born. There is still a long way to go for the poet as a guardian of the physical and metaphysical.

Rough Roads could be thought of as being the representation of the roads both taken and non-taken in life. In other words "the rough" is not just "the known" that has become familiar or experienced.

It could also be unforeseen the twists and turns one might ponder on. The rough might comprise the yet to come string of obstacles and predicaments one should be ready for, poetically and emotionally. In light of this, Man's image is observable in the bosom of time as though it were an elastic being on an endless onerous journey. Nevertheless, this work also contains poems as profound echoes of hope.

As usual my truly heartfelt thanks are due to my highly respected and valued publisher, Steve Wheeler for being a great support in the editing of this book.

Rafik Romdhani
Rakada, Tunisia
September 2022.

Muse is Sudden

Muse is absent or maybe late
busy somewhere and half-drunk.
I am here pondering fate,
upturning brains, ready to think.

Muse is sudden. No need to wait
or lose your time doing nothing.

The idle hours can give and take.
A humming fan is a trapped wing
in lower sky, closer to ache.

The heat of Kairouan, a cruel king,
the face of morning in hell's shape.
Even the sun ordering a drink,
flashing the ocean a witty wink.
I stir this coffee and ruminate
upon mind's ships in sweat lake.

Poetic thorns pricking my lung
and words begging to be sung.
From art's spell there is no easy escape.

In perfect profundity I'm flung
and at the invisible, my mouth agape.

Words

Words find their way out of the eye
prowling for the gyres in images
like frolicking flames above wet hay,
and beneath fresh bridges.
Words jilt the old meanings.
They wish them to waste away
like decomposing vapours,
before kissing the velvety sky.

Rogue Train

Rogue train!
You turn away and leave me alone
on the platform of memory,
picking up all the passengers at the stations
under the order of hurry.
You swallow all the pretty girls
and desperate suitcases like a hissing viper.
You are crushing words in the mind of a stone
thrown by a child at the tank of the occupier.
Yes, a stone left like a wish in the journey's valley,
like the breath that will rekindle the same fire.

Rogue train!
Are you ignoring me while on hope's wires
deep inside, thousands of birds are waiting,
White crows, sea-gulls, and a light-boned eagle
the size of a plane and the colour of an ember.
O fleeing wall to the whips of the wind
and weeping rain in the embrace of winter,
let me tell you that my ticked is reserved
and my suitcases are ready to wander.

Remember Rogue, that I am not an afterthought
or a mere dream given in to sharks by a sailor.
Rogue train!
I have my knives for the wildest distance,
for every neck drunk with nightmare.
I am aching lungs for the dust's calm nests.
You know, for the infinite I do have a flair.
I am all the passengers on criss-crossed pains
you may feel in fumes of railroads hung in the air.
Rogue train!

Thirsty Sponges

I sit here at my desk
waiting for the regular guest
to come: the night no doubt,
this less busy roundabout,
a hungry stranger
in the burning tent of the future.

A free blackness in the making
bullying the ember of dawn within.
Night's tall feet now wander,
Its dark clothes rarely shone.

I have nothing I should share
except the black waves of my hair.
Nothing to offer but the fate of words
under silence's stainless sword.

I sit here at my desk
drowning deep in Muse's cask
and ridding the hours of their masks.
Listening to the wind and barking dogs
that tear the clothes of flailing thoughts,
I put out each dying cigarette
in this cracked mug full of almond shells.
I welcome echoes from deep wells
and discuss with them the blues of the desert.

I sit here at my desk
Cause I am a night owl, a reaper of dusk.
I make sure all birds are asleep
then collect nightmares in one basket.

I'm a listening ear to rain when it starts to weep
I rest here for a moment
and carry on furrowing the heart
with poetry's plough.
What am I now gonna write about?

The absolute weeping of gods
or the thirsty sponges inside a poet?
I sit here at my desk
and into my mind a magical mirror has leapt.

What does this Morn want from Me?

What does this morn want from me?
It awakens the waves of sadness
and executes in my mouth an army of cigarettes.
The threads of light in front of the café
caressing the faces of passers-by
while the cold pen between my fingers
is waiting for what the mind is gonna say.
What does this morn want from me?
It promises my hands butterflies
exploring a garden in girls' hair
and opens my eyes on coffee blackness
where feelings could wander far.
What does this morn want from me?
It probably wants to shine brighter
in the soul and probe inside even more.

The Tribes of Despair

This poem hails from the tribes
of despair on the chest of my country.
I dedicate it to the packing silhouettes
catching thoughts' train and like me travelling.
It speaks of echoes deserting a deep sea,
of God's scribblings on the furrows of ships
and on splintering wrinkled faces.

This poem is a scream feeding on the angry,
a crawling soldier over slippery dunes
to reach the border of living meaning.
It is the broken knee from a corpse
clung to big blurry screens preening
in the interest of colourful promises
and drowning in sheer uncertainty to the ears.

This poem is the long hair of fire
you don't dare tie up or find one single buyer.
It speaks of twisted necks sprouting
from under cramming crowds ignored
and disappointment's heavy rocks.
It is the soul of birds leaving below the hurting.

This poem hails from the tribes
of despair on the chest of my country.
I dedicate it to the packing silhouettes
catching thoughts' train, and like me, travelling.

Rough Roads

In the bloom of burning absence
and the cold grip of unspoken-ness,
I wear the helmet of the night and consider.
Above me the jailed moon a blind cinder
contoured by biers made of clouds,
almost dead and waiting for the burial.

Both of us are amidst rough roads
wishing this murkiness to turn to a mural.
In the bloom of starving loneliness
swinging wide open worry's doors,
I welcome back my own sighs
that wind returns to me as an advice.

I stroke the dormant sand to explore words
and awaken the memory of ants
out of a sugar mound covered with salt.
Ants worship only sugar, this god of lust
all rejecting its sour brother by colour.
In the bloom of bones in circles of dust
above old cemeteries, I ponder
this orphan world where I am cast.

I gather the light gifts brought by wind,
the discarded leaves of mint,
the rolling dry shrubs hitting my shoulders,
the feathers after the crazy dance of birds.
In the bloom of teetering innocence
I bury myself inside the rambling void
and uproot hope from the back of verses.
The moon is hidden; it never chose to hide.
My hand bitten in the fading of moonlight,

I learn to no longer see space as mules do.
At dawn I'd take off the blinders of the night
and paint my grey ordeals sea-blue
for lost ships to sail and take me to you.

I store pain in my heart the way an ant so brave
stores rye grains in a forgotten grave
making a way with patience hard to subdue.
In the bloom of burning absence
and the cold grip of unspoken-ness,
I wear the helmet of the night and consider.

Above me the jailed moon a blind cinder
Contoured by biers made of clouds,
almost dead and waiting for the burial.
Both of us are amidst rough roads
wishing this murkiness to turn to a mural.

Desert Dancer

I don't see anything
except the dead wings
bombed by the unknown.
Who will caress Heaven's face
when birds die?
Who will live in me
when I can't find the words?
I don't see anything
in the valleys of wolves stuffed with void.
I don't hear anything
more than the echoes
carried by the blue back
of water that never looks back.
Who will hear me
when I'm with the dead
and in which language
will I write my verses?
I don't know anything.
I stand with time and place
In front of a huge mirror
made of grass and breaking waves.
I don't know anything but my name,
Yes, my arbitrary name with these
ridiculous limits that the body draws for me.
The desert is my exiled sister
that reminds me of the ships
of the night laden with loneliness.
I don't see anything in this silence
except a storm running through
my head like a desert dancer
scattering dust around me
and enlivening my senses.

Never Mind

Life! You vanquished me
in the first round
though I leaned back
on time's ropes
like a stubborn reed.

You vanquished me
and bombarded this mind
of mine with wishes
and daydreams.
Acting so weirdly,
you've got me spellbound,
and wound up with your mystery.

You knew which side
your bread- my blood-
is buttered and you devoured
the dream within the veins.
No one except you
taught this head
how to trap all the colours
in one rainbow
and all the breezes
in one window.

You vanquished me
in the first round.
That's true but I flourished
like a sun behind a cloud.
Your coldness made me
breathe winter before
I think of a fireplace,

taste the sweetness of grapes
before I enjoy it in bitter mugs
and thus I notice
the huge difference.

You vanquished me
in the first round
though I leaned back
on time's ropes
like a stubborn reed.

You were a harrowing war
and you still are,
including winners and losers.
I am but one
of the losers at a time
but not always,
a winner when all the buried
words in my ash choose to rise.

True, very true! You defeated me
and like a stone
you ignored every sound,
my voice, my scream,
my moan to the bone
in the remote forest of the mind.
I befriended your wolves.

That's also true,
wolves you delivered
and gave names to,
diurnal phantoms

you clothed in human flesh
and whom I wrongly try to hush
thinking they were humans.

I learnt from you through them,
drew on your tricks
and wallowed in your muddy face
like a migrating curlew
minding the fever of the unknown.

Oh life, I am a leap onto your stage
If you turn off the sun,
you can put me in a cage
all darkness sieging a man.

You vanquished me,
I had to bear you like no one.
But never mind I won't make any plea
Cause every day is a new round for me.

God Tell Me Why

Oh my God tell me why
She broke my heart
and held me at bay.
I saw love as an art
and thus been blown away.
Oh my God tell me why
I have no luck from the start.
She found home in my soul
and was safe from the cold,
yet ripped out all my veins
and with them built a masquerade.
Now she chooses to leave me
ignoring the dreams we once played.
Oh my God tell me why
how one can end an exquisite story
full of memories in the blink of an eye.
I was wrong placing trust
in a pigeon anytime ready to fly.
I was wrong in displaying the child inside
swinging the gate open this fast
for her fooling love that didn't last.
I was wrong with sounds from far and wide.
This I think but at times I do delve the snow's crust
flinging my heart like a ruby in her night.
Oh my God, tell me why
I have fallen as a prey to her tricks and fuzzy lies.
She was a liar I should have seen
with much more than my eyes.
She was a thief in relief,
and a punisher with impunity
for the love I gave and scribbled on every leaf.

Isn't Life a Jungle?

Isn't life a jungle
where some plant trust
and others sow wind
to reap nothing but dust?
Isn't it home for birds
and animals of all kinds,
home for clear vision within mist
and for injustice under sunlight?
Isn't life a jungle
where men's backs are sold
and bitten during tea time,
where the coward grow bold
at your iridescent worry on the mind?
Isn't life exempt from guilt
despite all the woven crimes
committed by pigs in human forms?
Isn't it where God has cast
you and me like breathing atoms,
where we stand alone
like trees on top of which the snow
lets go of its moan,
and mystery dwells like a crow
Isn't life a jungle
with all the chaos to handle,
where some plant trust
and others sow wind
to reap nothing but dust?

I Free Dreams

I free dreams on the mouths of bees
And nibble the tail of sweet worries.
Absence squeezes my blood like a lemon
I harvest waves to graft them on the breasts
of a woman drowning in love.

The distance between past and future
forever stretching, scattering memories
like spinning circles from above.
These knees I keep pushing towards
an elapsing mirage thereof
prove to be determined and stubborn.

I am a follower of visions and images.
I pick the thoughts of trees
growing in the form of luscious apples
and put them gently in fluttering hands.
I free my fingers in your hair
wishing them to die right there.

Love is Sailing on Your Lips

When I dream about you
the night always rages
like a train overdue
about to ride the waves.
When I dream about you
I live a million lives
telling the beads of morn dew.
The roses I water are love's hives
Where no soul feels blue.
When I dream I see my arms
like roots greening anew
amidst broken shards
giving dense shades
for the project of a curlew.
The brink of madness,
no one but you.
How can I explain our oneness
while you think we are two?
How can I accept a bleeding absence
with widening wounds hard to sew?
When I dream about us
I see nests being built on a nice view
and love sailing on your lips
like a ship on its own without a crew.

Mulberries

Mulberries are dangling nipples
from heaven,
great glittering diamonds.
They redden
to sunlight and darken to the night.

I see them as bullets
with which I kill the bile in this heart
where they tumble down like fingers
rescuing the croaking crows inside,
creatures wearing the coat of darkness
nesting here in the windows of the mind.

Each morn, they nurse desires
and on my bitter blood open their fires.
Mulberries fall down to the scythe of wind.
I collect them like war refugees in my hand
through watery depths where dust shall end.

Mulberries are never forbidden nipples
in the Garden of Eden.
You can bite torment now and then
and graft them on life's stinging thistles.

The Tomb of Memory

Life stretches out a white hand
from the tomb of memory
beckoning to me
as if I had to understand
that the morning rose is gone
and its thorns splashed into the mind
like a phoenix's skeleton
on a fiery mountainside.
Life stretches out a grey hand
where a spider has woven its dream
and magic chosen not to be seen.
But I know I'll be blamed at the end
for the crash of clouds on the top of a tree
and be held responsible for all the cries
as I am the only one who survives
well like a screaming philosophy.
I cry like I am the brother of loss
knowing death the first day of my life.
My wagon of worries I have to acquiesce
and print the moans a prisoner may shelf.
Life stretches out a purple hand
from the caves of a danger
stroking agony in gory land
and turning graves to lumps of sugar.
I'm floating here on my own dust
clutching to this strange hand
and fixing the face of the sand
that God has randomly tossed.
Life stretches out a white hand
from the tomb of memory
beckoning to me
as if I were an old friend.

Days Are Random Butterflies

Days are random butterflies.
Sometimes they perch on carnations
and some other times
are carried towards breezy destinations
to be thrown on a wall
without a soul or a smell.

Days are wagons with wings,
You have but to follow their journeys
and wait for the surprise
they are opening before your eyes.

You can burst now in tears
of joy but tomorrow you may capsize
alone in a frozen lake full of bears.
Days are famished arrows
targeting the tails of tomorrows.
You had better not face them
like a hollow skull at their front.

But be the wizard from behind.
Scratch the neck of each moment
with the tip of your pen
and fill in the spots on either side.
Days are random butterflies
easy to catch but hard to ride.

My Heart is a Seashore

My heart is a seashore.
Fabulous beauties, sweet guests
In full spring, it wants more
and a spell on all it often casts.
My heart is a seashore
and at your presence becomes a vase.
I do feel your touch to the core
thrilled by those bare feet in their pause.

My heart is a seashore
where the ships of love worry no more.
These waters without you start to be rough
breaking all the bridges inside on your behalf
driving me down like a seed of madness
locked up in strange depths with no door.
I am a seashore where waves bite the dust
before reaching your face I more than adore.

The Wounds You Sew

Don't disappear like a sea in a mirror
and leave the sand without a painter
to pull the depths out of a glass of beer
and play havoc with pure colors.
Don't run like a river in the ocean
of dry grass.
for you know you won't salvage
dreams without thirst.
Don't disappear like a tattered coat
on the back of a stranger
in a market crammed with customers.
Sobs will find a way to your throat.
Your own shadow will stab you inside
a pack of busy wolves around.
Absence will crush you like a grape
a bereaved mother put on her son's tomb
for the diamond light of the moon.
Don't look through others' eyes
at your lemon tree embracing the sun
Cos you will pick the diaphanous skies
and cut the cascading hair of rain.
Don't disappear like a sea under mist
when storms surround you
like a huge pile of days hard to resist.
Don't reopen the wounds you sew.
Don't disappear in them like a sea in a mirror
and leave the sand without a painter
to pull the depths out of a glass of beer
and play havoc with pure colors.

A Hell Too Hot to Deaden

It was a night so bleak, so sad
When I got up to the ringtones of mourning.
Mom was crying a river.
On her back, my brother
sweating from fever and vomiting
out life thorn by thorn.

We brought his cat as it was his only concern
Yet to it he did not turn his head
unable to notice its caressing against his arm
or feel the meowing that rocks him to bed.
This world is cruel enough to do me harm.

The friendly voice forever would be gone
He knew nothing of what it means to be dead.
Too young to be informed about death's call.
I rose from my sleep both appalled and mad
My ears, a huge stage for tragedy's free fall.

We used to play near the streak
in front of old houses built of straw and mud
where the wind blows adjusting its strings.
Sweet memories came like arrows to the mind.

We collected crickets in empty bottles
and buzzing bees of all the kinds
All the good things with water went away
I thought that the elderly only were to die
But it seems that death could rob you
of the only peer with whom you play
and break bread you share joyfully and chew.

We used to have fun taking the eggs
of a dove and putting them in a crow's nest.
We would do the same thing to the poor crow.

The result is utter confusion at its best
and a charade like life itself
when shocking feathers begin to show
and the fooled dove is played off against a foe.

We used to laugh like the sun
and run like the wind that dances with dust.
My brother is now in Heaven
but I'm down a hell too hot to deaden.

Bite Before You Write

Bite the neck of the void
Bite your pencil or pen,
the tail of thoughts in the mind.
Bite your pain from now and then.
Bite despair like a white bear
finding his image in dancing cloud
sieged by wind up there.
Bite the dark in the eyes of the blind.
Bite your fingers, write with their blood.
Bite the ears of all the fools waging war.
Bite even with more than your teeth
the growing roots underneath.
Bite before you write
the lazy lady supine on the stage
Bite life into her and rage
at your heavy night.

I Sleep Outside My Grave

My feet are wandering a weird land.
They never see ashes as the end.
I disappear like luck
but I know when to come back.
The sky is an eternal bird ahead,
distributing its feathers among the seasons.
I keep pondering and disobeying my head,
My feet are two ants caressing the wet lips
of the sand dreaming of shoes from clouds
I disappear as a face in disdain.
I sleep outside my grave unlike everyone else
but like a river with its mouth open to the rain.

My Night is Long

My night is long without cigarettes
to console me.
A lantern hangs over my thoughts
like a daisy.
Or like a man hanged by the unknown.

There is a terrible silence around me,
an immense void, and a tough burden.
Where are you now, my love?
I looked for you under the sea
and in almond roses.

I only saw your bosom heavy with fruits
My night is as long as a mountain range
I am tired and under my feet a thorny page.
A thousand bags on these shoulders
against the wall's awakened bones.

Come to me, my distant eye;
I would love to smoke your fingers
like a child and heave this repressed sigh.
My night is long without cigarettes.
Let me pick dreams from your gypsy hair.

Is there any place in you to bury despair?
Come to me, my breeze.
The pillow of the sea I drew
on the ceiling is waiting for you
all drenched in tears.

My poem will go everywhere
searching for an end to our war.

My poem wants a dance from you
before it takes off above heart's land.
My night is long without cigarettes
and still longer than your absence,
my unique mirror!

If you don't come, this black wolf
this killing dark will tear me down
to love you on my behalf
and I'll succumb to its scornful laughter.

A Cry in the Sky

A cry in the sky would gather
broken foxes and wolves
hares with no shelter
and shattered partridges.
A cry in the sky startling the void
awakening my dreams.
My ears are two deer
petrified by the roars of the mind
bearing with me the drumming
of demons and the grievances
that angels are nursing.
A cry in the sky speaks of evanescence
exploding the sounds inside our heads,
the pink lamps of light in pomegranate roses.
Birds hatch the planet each spring in their eggs
and bathe like dreamers in their nests.
A cry in the sky disperses the specks of dust
to clear the way towards the shores of trust
and symbiosis you can feel in the unity
of waters in an ocean and the beauty
of nature in its soothing silence.
A cry in the sky would gather
floating dreams and galloping thoughts
under God's limitless umbrella.
The whisper of the moon breaking
clouds in halves
to see us dreamy and hugging
like two ships brought closer by waves.
A cry in the sky would gather
broken foxes and wolves
hares with no shelter
and shattered partridges.

The Eye of God

Who would wash the face
of the desert apart from cold rain?
Who would dare to descend
from a well dug by prayers in the sky
to sweep away the sorrow of the sand?
Who would plough the scattered paths
on a broad picture other than the mules
of memory that drag spring behind them
and trample the fierce thorns
sucking the soil's blood?
Who would build tents and grow tendrils
for the coming shadows
From thoughtful twilights
and fragrant flowers for bees?
No one weeps for your soaring skin
in the form of dust of Mother Earth
thrown into space, except golden rain.
Who would remove the needles of pain
aside from the eye of God with its worth.

Oubliette of the Sea

At the bottom of the sea
the sun blows out
its hot flames,
and sleeps like a bride
waiting for her adorned day
with daffodils.
At the bottom of the sea
The night pours out its pain
bathed in sour tears
and paints itself black
from the water's darkness.
At the bottom of the sea
poetry sinks like an immigrant
trusting everything,
everything without precaution.
At the bottom of the sea
I find the sky's mirror and the wind's hair
Kept safe and given care.
But I didn't find myself.
I am an echo through a journey
in the deep roots of water,
a silhouette in the oubliette of the sea.
I didn't find an answer...
No, I didn't.

Windows

I didn't know windows had wings
floundering in the winds
managing to flee away like prisoners
with salty nightmares on their lips.
I didn't know that cement block walls
and locked iron doors
are abhorrent to the point of tears.
I didn't know, my peers
that windows fast all night,
starve and open their mouths
during the day to rain and dust
like baby doves being fed by mothers.
I didn't know that dawn comes
from the window like an orange
ripening on the face of darkness
to be shared by varied sponges,
like an ember whose goal is space
and life's ephemeral fringes.
I didn't know that walls could sense
doom when a window cringes.
A window awaits the arrival of two girls,
barefooted, blood covering their toes.
Windows are severe wounds in stones,
semi-open graves for the beloved ones
buried with oblivion, no peep-holes or windows
I didn't know windows had wombs
where dream develops and grows
like a caterpillar in a cocoon that God sows
and turns to a butterfly, tangled up in perfumes.

Crows Carry the Sky

On their backs
crows carry the sky
ignoring the wind's attacks
that may impugn their way.
On their backs
life decides the birth of the sun
after the fall of darkness
and the perishing of the moon.
On their backs
crows build bridges and rainbows
that I can't be put into words
or materialize into pithy volumes.
On their backs
God's messenger reads passages
from sacred books
all meanings and adages.
On their backs
crows carry the sky
and its voluptuous vaults
further than you could cast your eye.
On their backs
a bard burns and pauses,
sings and walks
breathing lives into gargoyles.
On their backs
crows carry dawn's face
to future's long arms
outstretching for it in an embrace.

Our Songs are all Alone

The images of life blown,
huddling in the darkness
of the unknown
clinging to the wind's face
in rebellion.

Days are so far away behind
running like starving hyenas
after our heartbeat.
The future is a broken father
beclouded in fog.
Stars a crazy translation
of the spawn of many a frog.

The longest distance
is deep inside within us.
It takes miles for emotions
to burst into shivers
on a dry mouth.
We never see our faces
Not even in a wall mirror.

We never see them on the face
of clean water.
They are deeper than the sea
and farther than the sky.
The images of life blown,
huddling in the darkness
of the unknown
clinging to the wind's face
in rebellion.

We trust the teeth of time
no more though we try.
The loudest cry
of a curlew is a knife
slashing silence in dismay.
We sing our guts about life
but our songs are all alone
crossing the ocean
never returning to our throats.

After Three Cigarettes

After three cigarettes
I have in a rush
I glance at shining stars
bathing in ash
I see my room's curtains
blanching into shrouds
and windows behind them
yawning like open coffins.
After three cigarettes
my head sends
strange sounds
much like railway wagons.
My thoughts wandering,
plodding incredible miles.
Ah! I shan't reopen
the wound of spring.
No, I shan't touch
the face of the moon
or scratch
it as it falls down in a swoon
inside an ocean.
After three cigarettes
I toke like a fool
I turn my back to darkness,
to life's whirlpool
laying down the suitcases
of a heart so laden, so full
on a burning floor.
Ah! I won't measure
the bust of emptiness
nor plough the fields
I see in fertile mirror.
No I won't.

I clamp my cigarettes
between my index
and my middle finger
like I am dealing with prisoners,
and I inhale the nebular night
with its secrets and mysteries.
After three cigarettes
I open wide my eyes,
freeing all detained sighs
like a chest owing time huge debts.

A Candelabrum Behind Bars

I can gather passing clouds,
make them weep in a poem.
Rivulets would be free lines
I can't help but welcome.
I can push the walls around
me to shake off their memories
and speak those minds out loud
they haven't spoken for centuries.
I'm wise enough in the ways of fools.
I create a dying life like the one
we are all living, a life that hope fuels.
I can plough the journey begun,
just like dew beads on lonely roses,
and let in the lame shadows of absence.
I'm a candelabrum behind bars
painting an epidermis aloof from stars.
I'm a hand holding the shards of loss
and the snow of December.
I can teach the dead how to remember
the tears on their dormant course.
At my behest the night's head lowers
as if to soak in the showers of oblivion
and swim in my eyes like a mad woman.
I can aid her tear off her black curtains
sewn by the sharp needles of rains.
I can gather waves in my coffee mug,
and like a desert in need of a hug
I'd thirst for them till no wave remains.
I can gather passing clouds,
make them weep in a poem.
Rivulets would be free lines
I can't help but welcome.

Eerie Silence

Night dips its daggers
in the back of the moon
in eerie silence.
Wishes sleep wrapped
in their moans like fingers
caressing a poem's wound,
like soldiers without minds
returning from the void.
Night dips its daggers
in the eye of a dream
causing wolves to howl
without any guilt
as if they were grievances
that heaven ignored
grievances only stone and trees
have borne for years and years.
Night dips its daggers
in the first cloud
which bitterly cries
drenching pillows
ocean-size
and in halves
breaking our souls.
Night dips its daggers
in the back of the moon
in eerie silence.

Heart Desert

You wish to carry my corpse
on your cold shoulders
and bury my eyes
in their own tears you cause.

You wish to glean my dreams
in one single sapphire
and dance like demons
brought to life by fire.

You wish to haunt my mirror
after I am no more
to see if I still have the vigour
I used to have before.

You wish to pick the sun
the way you pick a lemon
How dare you orphan dawn
after unsheathing your weapon!

You wish to grow the moon
in your inner darkness.
The bust of the azure will soon
turn beamless.

You chase your own behoves
howling loud like wolves.
You wish to carry my coffin
all lofty and laughing,

You wish to share the ocean
while I moan and croon.

Thoughts from frenzy I fashion
are waterfalls in June.

You wish to read the pages
I have written in blood
and kept unread within ribs
but studded playfully with mud.

You wish to dig me a tomb
in your heart desert,
cut my throat with thirst,
and leave me no wish to climb.

City of Cement

No insidious faces, no pain
in the cement city
No haste, no worry
about what we cannot explain.
In the cement city
no fake laughing with the teeth
while setting traps underneath
No hocus-pocus or trickery.
Only souls validated by the Deity
rendering to earth its clay.
What in life was a reality
is now a dream drifting away.
The eye of wind may know the way
of the bygone moment with the gone.
No vein retain at smothering the sun.
Yet still there is breath though bones grey
as lanterns paddle along the dark.
There are lights and godly wires
But only the living receive the shock
for their instincts and desires.
In the city of cement
We meet ourselves after long absence
abandoning these cages to ferment
as we sleep long, steeped in silence.

Poetry Slays All Sacred Cows

When life hatches its crows
and wind heaves its wheeze
Poetry slays all sacred cows
censuring dogma as it pleases.
When water chooses to freeze
I look for it in water weeds.
Life's shadow comes and goes
leaving behind rivers of tears.
The face of memory pain draws
speaks volumes no one knows.
In their sting, days hide tails like bees
from whose mouths honey flows.
The under-thoughts that nights sows
may stretch roots like trees
through a journey of whys and hows.
But as more horror gathers and grows
to bring the mind to its knees,
the valour of verse in heart blows
and homes the heaven that hope frees.

White Waves above the Sea

What could these fumes be taking out
with them from me
as they journey way ceiling through mouth
like a white mythology?
Maybe this head is a wizard amidst blizzard
boiling things I can't see.
Maybe that's the way musings should be,
foggy like fantasy flying un-scissored.
Are they the hair of a woman that hides inside
with coming echoes in the night only I confide?
Where could this transience be leading me
while it gathers around hauntingly?
Maybe I am the sky of warbirds
crashing into a pond of rippling words
leaving nothing more than ash and fumes.
Maybe I am the desert's palm before it blooms.
What could these phantoms be taking out
with them from me
other than the too many queries to count
hung like white waves above the sea.

The Embers of the Sand

I am my own different path
I twist the tedious times,
suck avidly the breast of death
dipping my hand in tepid wines.
I twist the tedious times,
I melt brokenness with heartburn
dipping my hand in tepid wines
vomiting the galls that hotly churn.
I melt brokenness with heartburn
like a camel crushing the desert with its knees
vomiting the galls that hotly churn
in a smouldering hell without a breeze.
Like a camel crushing the desert with its knees
I pillow my head on the embers of the sand
in a smouldering hell without breeze
and gaze into faces too shadowy to understand

Dust Reunion

On the eyelids of the sun falls the night
despondent but glad with the warmth
it feels from hunching fright
above lonely ships returning from death.
On the eyelids of the sun dies the dark
with the image of a wheat sheath
in a farmer's hand as light as a paper dart
among white angels in disbelief.
The night, this cold beggar clad in black
with beseeching stars and battling waves beneath
wants nothing more than to unpack
the queuing questions that you breathe.
On the eyelids of the sun roses grieve
the loss of butterflies beyond retrieve.
Our faces half-dead in lamb-wool pillows
torn between soft dreams and nightmares.
God is half-crying and half-laughing
in the middle between hell and paradise,
wiping the tears of the sky and on the sun
putting radiant kisses through frozen ice.
On the eyelids of the sun drunken brains
see scars much like black coffee stains.
No one is blind for inside many a mirror
is giving light but seldom the shivers.
On the threshold of patience violet wings
waiting to rise and fly above the base.
Infinite space ahead like a soothing place
for dust's reunion in desert's blooming.
On the eyelids of the sun falls the night
floored and fooled by the neck of distance
it can ride no more or halt for a moment
to dictate the diction of doom and pass.

The Last Bird

By the end of spring
most flowers wilt and fall,
Wind blows to say nothing
like a wizard's hollow call.
By the end of spring
surges a thirsty painter
ordered by the sun to sing
and start the de-colouring.
A gothic mouth yawning
descends as a returned ember
to Nature where it has to cling.
Bloodless veins do shudder
at war's red lakes now filling.
By the end of spring
birds in the soul only find nesting
and like words make the unseen picture.
The story of ash in the beaks of crows.
They relate it in anguish to oleander,
which is why the latter tastes bitter.
By the end of spring you find your foes
watering life's thorns with more than water
not sleeping their nightmares, cunning
like pieces of shade scattered by wonder.
Madness begins as a window in a mountain
letting in ghosts shepherded by the wind.
By the end of spring
ugliness unfeathers the jubilant flower
saps the sand's froth that memories still embower.
By the end of the end,
weird creatures take a stand as they hover
like heat vowing to eat the last grain at hand,
the last sky for the last bird I wish to colour.

65

The Pomegranate of Possibilities

You thought you killed me
and on my tomb you came dancing,
to the dark making a plea
pulling the carpets from under my feet
to ascertain more this vanishing.

You thought this dormant hand
didn't paginate the chapter of suffering
you had inflicted forgetting.
I have long been a friend,
an old friend with falling and rising.

You thought the sky wouldn't lift the sun
and create below it a quicksand
that would swamp you down one by one.

I'm here above you where I should stand.
I empathize with the graves you dug
as you bury in them nothing but your disdain.
A wonderful laughter shares with me my mug
of hope, my clear vision, my final aim.

You thought you shrouded me
Yet around me life's lips are blossoming,
brushing against mine like the mouth of a bee.
Only the lunatic describe tired fingers resting
as death and to the dark make a plea
to ascertain in your evil eye a presumed dying.

You thought I wouldn't cogitate infinitely
You thought.

The pomegranate of possibilities is opening
like rain from the void you hear tapping
on your coward cemeteries of the mind
Don't be frightened; I'm not a ghost chasing
you as much as your own mirror from behind.

You thought you had banished me.
Now to my world you come whining,
to your remorse begging the sea
to wash away your evil doing.
You thought...

No One

No one writes about the sun
while it is waiting for us
on the other side of confusion.
Far away out there behind
the mountains of madness.
We stare into the mirrors
of each other's faces
like dumb questions
feeding on the murder of meanings
hiding under the wing of blackness.
No one speaks of dawn
and its luminous redness
riding distance like a wounded man.
Play to me and now, you rain drops
leaking from a ceiling so divine yon,
my ears died in my last battle
with the sounds of wolves going on
The night is as long as my cigarette tail.
I'm still far away
behind the mountains of madness.
I sit here calmly on anxiety's hills
envisioning the ships of the sea
as if I were one among the starving seagulls.
No one writes about what he cannot see
as the sky descends with its blind curtains,
as waves return defeated, like Roderic's army.
I'm still far away but facing invisibility.
No one climbs the abstruse necks
of the impossible and writes out light
the moment light is under the rubble so sick.
As the long hours play their treat or trick
I hunker down to receive the first beam
with patient eyes brimming with dream.

Dreamscape

Dry Eucalyptus leaves thicken my tea,
my black mirror, my ease of mind
in the cup bottom waiting for me.
Wreaths of smoke almost intertwined
take my breath in their stride.
Angst and agony shall cease and flee
Or I'll sip them and breathe out poetry.
My cup of tea for thoughts unmined
gazing like an eye that mustn't be blind,
which is why I think that objects may see
and have emotions in forms undefined,
which is why I possess any kingdom's key.
My hunger for thinking blackens my sea,
my subliminal dreamscape so easy to find
from the surface down the wits of tea.
My lips on the rim, my eyes going down
exploring my fantasy and searching for me.
Yet a big part has departed with the wreaths
far above the night like a glistening galaxy.
What stays are verses to you a poet bequeaths.

I Don't Write Anything

I don't write anything.
The things around are what defines me.
Letters jump like gerbils,
dig holes in the mind, and grow into words,
shrieking words gasping for eternity.

I don't write anything
My feelings wake me up every night
while trotting backwards inside my ribs
like untamed horses, writing me and sticking
my dreams to their swimming backs.

I don't write anything
My cigarette and wine ignite my cogitation
and outflank my head like two goddesses
Demanding the ambrosia of verses.

Smoke wreaths are ropes about my neck
acting like guillotines from metaphysics.
Wine slowly kindles my chest and writes
the gut-wrenching scenes of wreck.

I don't write anything.
The dawn besmeared with the blood
of the innocent, and the white sun
ashamed of man's hatred
for his fellow man,
are witnesses to the echoes of the explosions.

Each dawn paints my eyes on its hot redness,
and the sun melancholically writes the sweat
of disappointment on my invaded forehead.

I don't write anything
My fingers become bayonets steeped in regret,
not wanting to bleed my heart through the pen.

My hands chase the first cloud on life's chest
Leaving me armless and jailed like a mad man.
The windowpanes of the soul so cold and shut
mirroring a blanket of fog shrouding the sun.

Today is Your Day

Today is your day, my blood.
I see children as light as butterflies
crossing the borders of darkness.
They are all aches and echoes.

The last song died on their lips
like a light extinguished in the midst of dust.
Today is your day, my poem
coming from the twilight of madness.

Speak of crazy times like a stone
getting along pretty well with waters.
Speak of crimes that in mind should be borne.

Today is your day, my hand
to lock up all the demons
in a dungeon and measure the huge bust
of non-blessed drudgery of free men.

Today is your day, my bottles
to empty my chest of moans
and cut ghosts' arteries on the barbed wire.

Rip my veins for in my blood
there are encrypted messages, and lost ships
not knowing how to return near sea pier,
near its fingers that flirt with the sand.

Today is your day to dream all of just one land.
A wandering mind turns a lofty page
the size of a wave victims' backs must stand.

Today is your day, my pen to liberate
an army of throats in one single poem
but their rebellion, don't think to abate.
Let them scream out the morbid tone.

Today is your day to kindle your fire
out of its dormant ashes.
Many a soul silence slashes
and offers as gift to vampires.

Unknowable nightmares chasing dreams
like shrouds of snow woven in space
and crashing into life's thrashed face.

Changes are chances coming your way
because today is simply your day.

The Banners of Love and Peace

Show the world, the entire world
you won't play with death anymore
nor kindle the unforgiving fires of war.
Innocence splinters under your sword
and mothers pillow their heads no more.
Show the Lord, the merciful Lord
not all human deeds are to abhor.
Without peace nothing adorable will be adored.
Show Him the banners of love and peace.
The hell of winter in children's knees
piling the pale toys of torment.
Isn't it wiser to have war funds on life spent?
Isn't it better to open divine windows
in the bosom and think no ill, my friend?
You think Heaven's vaults without you would close
and you lock up sylphs with the key in your hand.
You water death with guiltless blood
and startle dreams out of their bed!
Place your hands on the shoulders of trees
Free the laughter of the wind and the whisper of breeze.
Be lubricated with the cups of searing tears.
Just turn those guns into candelabra,
War is night in daylight feasting upon our fears.
Sob stories in throats throttled beyond horror.
Show the world, the entire world
you won't indulge in blood baths anymore
nor go berserk like Poe's Montresor,
whose inner workings by degrees unfurled.

Love's Applause

Come on my blonde rose;
let's put the night in a bottle
we've drunk together in harmony's applause.
Come, butterfly on the shoulder of the wind,
I need you by my side and in my inked page
for it is your mirror and soul's sand.

Come on and wait for me
like you don't wait for me.
I'm coming and the world is in my hand.
Just let me twist the neck of darkness
and with the threads of rain descend
so that the river between your breasts
will flow forever as if there were no end.
I'm hovering like a dream to have the cosmos
explode inside of you like the moribund.

Come on my blonde;
Come on my blonde rose,
Let's put the night in a bottle
we've drunk together in love's applause.

Budding Hearts Faint in Venom

Love without sacrifices
from the start, just throw.
You're only worth a few words
one writes by the hand or draws.
Love is locked in lies you know
and imprisoned in demon figures
who at the dream's space gnaw
like cruel hounds no one fathers.
Love without sacrifices,
just leave behind and let go.
Everything is loss
and everyone in limbo.
Dream towers built are now fallen.
Budding hearts faint in venom
like bleeding history on a red rock.
Life laughs first then starts to mock
and in one blink casts its fiery billow
tracking you down to get you trodden.
Love outside sanity is but an illusion.
No one can give, or out of monstrosity burrow.

Beside the Shards of Beer Mugs

Things are no longer what they used to be.
The rose did not complete her run
with the butterflies.
She did not complete her spring rhapsody.
Fire battering like a wave in its place
fearing the frenzy of water
under the dreaming tombs.
Things are no longer what I used to see
and breathe in avidly.
Those guiding faces toward light are no more.
My soul went south and won't return
I no longer inhabit this body,
but I think I should visit it
like death stealthily
I get closer to this phantom
singing to ward off obscurity.
I run away like a cigarette to my fingers
which is liberated in its burning.
Burn my princess burn I came here for learning
Things are no longer what they used to be
Life no more taps at my eyes in the morning
Memory is a crow changing into mythology
predicting what is unknowable to me.
I'm a page on the edge of imagery
the breath putting out the incinerator on ice.
I hate fire being lit before children
and wept over by their eyes,
and my sighs I find broken
beside the shards of beer mugs?
I will collect them to build with solid piers.
Things are no longer what they used to be
Dust ceased moving around clouds
and covering the bust of the universe.

I Build Poems

I build poems from a soul's inspiration
sweat beads jutting on my forehead.
When like lightning my life flashes
I wear the sun on my skin half-dead.
Heat in hope I embed and fast take action.
Like a mason cutting stones blue and red,
I cut images and haemorrhage this flood.
I build poems around a question
and thatch their sky with the unsaid
to save spring from cyclones.
I build poems for the living and the dead.
My only aspirin is aspiration with light bones.
I build, I build poems no queen condones
or gets under the sway of passion.
But I'll explode more and home hushed tones.

One Day I Will Sleep Long

I know one day I will sleep long
And the sky will be reduced to the grave's ceiling
That I will think aloud like no one is hearing
On a pillow as light as a song.
I know I will depart
And the wind will knock on my door.
The night will tiptoe through every pore
publishing the halted poetry in my heart.
I know death will tie my hands
to a floating ship built from bones
and ride a sea wept by souls
that life scatters and eternal sleep gathers.
I know I will die to finish my dreams,
write dusty poems, and change the themes.

Blind Destiny

Come down your high horse, Blonde!
and if I stop you for a moment don't bother.
You are in haste trotting like a moon
and escaping clouds one after the other.

Tell me how you feel
in this void away from the commune
with your chin-up attitude
Tell me how this heart can heal
and be filled with plenitude
without you being ever near.

You choose silence and journey
but your absence leaves me in no mood.
I shut my eyes on your peerless beauty.
I shut the doors and the windows
of each and every room
to find you and me side by side,
Our heads on two envious pillows.

I empty my ears of the venom of time
and the tumult of gloom,
soak each ear like a golden dime
in your deepening dreams.

Now I find you jilted by the unknown,
your feet bare for the tongue of rain
while you are riding your shivering bones.
Now we won't roam this earth in vain.

Your fingers are mint roots drowning
in my diluting patience,
outgrowing themselves

to become hugging arms.
My fingers dream of your face
and fly like nightingales
that every morn on your window sill perch
I'll always be waiting for you here
on the side of the road, my dear
at the old railway station built by the French.

I'll always be waiting for you here.
I will free my heart of this damned witch
and be all space for you each time you appear.
Here on these walls I will write your name
so that the train recalls all the girls
who inflamed the hearts of men for no aim.

I will always be waiting for you.
Your love will crush me
without damaging any vein
Your love is the train
and the blind destiny.

I will always be waiting for you.

The Brink and the Fall

Behind me is the depth of the night
and the moaning of graves.
The red sun burnt away in its flight
like a honeycomb drained by knaves.
The world burns on an unseen fire
like the hurt, invisible yet stings.
Behind me these walls' desire
for more stupendous songs.
I wander the busy streets of the heart
waltzing with rising emotions
and waiting for the first light.
I did not know that dawn comes
from patience and sacrifices so great.
I realized I am down a road full of dramas
written by God and played by fate.
Behind me are budding dreams
in a memory's grey nests
and in spiders' wicked webs .
Dreams are mothers of butterflies,
the reason why the fool may turn wise
at times and shine among stars
Behind me dull moments in busy bars,
Blind thoughts revolving around my mind.
There are hesitant mirrors that time did ride.
Behind me the wind like a lie
preparing the whips of torment.
My shadow has become a spy
following me like an absent present.
Dust wrapping me and acting as a bier
in the sphere of the void.
Behind me the globe, this big blue tear
and the stubs of my cigarettes, buoyed
in a hasty river rich in stones.

Behind me the corpse of the impossible
bleeding and water exploding in moans.
Behind me the moon centering a dark ocean,
desperate dogs coming to sniff my footprints
in a writhing desert and bark at nothing
except the terrible claws of torment.
Behind me the broken circles of sandstorms,
weary wings in their ascent to the Milky Way.
Behind me the whole cosmos a cold snowball
But I do feel the warmth from your azure eyes
bring me back from both the brink and the fall.

The Tribes of Despair

This poem hails from the tribes
of despair on the chest of my country.
I dedicate it to the packing silhouettes
catching thoughts' train and like me travelling.
It speaks of echoes deserting a deep sea,
of God's scribblings on the furrows of ships
and on splintering wrinkled faces.
This poem is a scream feeding on the angry,
a crawling soldier over slippery dunes
to reach the border of living meaning.
It is the broken knee from a sad corpse
clung to big blurry screens preening
in the interest of colourful promises
and drowning in sheer uncertainty to the ears.
This poem is the long hair of fire
you don't dare tie up or find one single buyer.
It speaks of twisted necks sprouting
from under cramming crowds ignored
and disappointment's heavy rocks.
It is the soul of birds leaving below the hurting.
This poem hails from the tribes
of despair on the chest of my country.
I dedicate it to the packing silhouettes
catching a thought's train and like me, travelling.

If I Only Knew

If I knew life was a chimney
hidden behind the white teeth
of light pouring on its folly
the oil of death and grief,
If I knew it was as rough
as swine skin or hard beef
no furnace digests enough
with the stomach of heat,
If I knew these faces
around that angels evade
are but flesh coins God tosses
on the stage of masquerade,
If I knew that the wicked
reference God's word the most
and give ear to the gossip of wind
beneath the walls of void as grey ghosts,
If I knew existence was exegesis
of perpetuated shadows
with long flat feet to crush aspirations
for an illusion so luscious,
If I knew you were breeders of good evil
and blind minds before waterfalls,
I would behave otherwise
and try dwelling the highs like an eagle.

An Army of Skeletons

I hear the squelch of feet as they tread
on the eyelids of the earth
igniting the rose petals with red,
blue, and yellow fire and warmth.
Night flies and disappears
in the face of the sun.
Life comes like a mare
accustomed to the dust's dress.

The terrifying scarecrows
inhabit wheat fields
and respond like faithful fans to wind.
Girls' laughter embellishing their mouths
sound like the fluttering of young fledged birds
about to wander and aspire to every cloud.

An army of skeletons singing life
on their way to the arms of death.
I hear the wagons of moans
coming out from the diaphanous horizon.
A whole world is departing and moving.

The scream of God awakens thyme perfume
and feasts upon the limitless road in my eyes
before which days have much more to exhume.
An invisible temptress takes me by the hand
as we cross the penetrable body of the void.

We don't know where we're going.
We don't know who we are.
Fate borrowed our memories,
burdened our feet and ordered us to leave.

I hear the squelch of feet as they tread
on the eyelids of the earth
igniting the rose petals with red,
blue, and yellow fire and warmth.
Night flies and disappears
in the face of the sun.

Spring Won't End

The image of roses will remain
here stuck in every mirror,
in every rippling face of water
melting in the thrumming rain.
Spring won't end with May.
Petals of hope, celestial vapour.
Spring won't end with the harvest
of waves that autumn scythes
wildly and commences to cast.
The blue of the sea will climb
the mountain and blow away my mind.
It will paint the bust of the sky,
this blue bird with eternal wings
carrying the wind's cold sigh
and the wrath of the sun.
Spring won't end with the hatching of eggs
and the silence of crickets in daytime.
Songs will continue to numb
the sober ear of the night.
Cages will be whistling chests for the breeze.
Spring won't end with the undressing of trees.
Birds will shake off snow and stupor,
Roses will bloom in the hand of a dead child
and in the thirst of a woman for going wild.
Spring won't end.
Cactus roses will be lampposts for my dreams
and amazingness in the memory of bees.
Spring won't end.
The image of roses will remain
here stuck in every mirror,
in every rippling face of water
melting in the thrumming rain.

The Ribs of a Legend

The sea was born from repetitive blows
of an axe in the mirror of the sky.
Earth receives tears the size of waves.
Wind breaks out like a stormy sigh
yearning for the necks of mountains.
History runs like a mare's heart
on the ground of Greek philosophers
hungry for the poetry of Homer.
Mind-invaded utopia collapses
and dies like soothing smiles
on the mouths of dead soldiers.
The mind born out of a seed of doubt
in the eye of a crow who built
his nest from cow dung and mud
and peeled the sun as if it were an olive
varnishing its wings with light.
Abundance of miscellaneous gods
on every side no one ignores.
The brother of death pulling down
its curtains on living eyes.
Days are snakes leaving their skin
on the sand to dupe the sun of August.
They offer their sharp fangs like needles
for the frozen imagination under snow.
Night is a towering pile of undreamt dreams.
Dawn is the red place of a bullet pulled out
from the back of darkness
A poem could be the last bullet
targeting the head of disappointment
and creating cracks in the ribs of a legend.

Love is Sailing on Your Lips

When I dream about you
the night always rages
like a train overdue
about to ride the waves.
When I dream about you
I live a million lives
telling the beads of morn dew.
The roses I water are love's hives
Where no soul feels blue.
When I dream I see my arms
like roots greening anew
amidst broken shards
giving dense shades
for the project of a curlew.
The brink of madness,
no one but you.
How can I explain our oneness
while you think we are two?
How can I accept a bleeding absence
with widening wounds hard to sew?
When I dream about us
I see nests being built on a nice view
and love is sailing on your lips
like a ship on its own without a crew.

Bridge Over Logic

I held space in my right eye
and proffered my left one as a spare wheel
for the wagons of time.
Now distance means nothing to me.
Down within lie the ends of the unknown
and the smart soul of the Infinite,
the Occident and the Orient.
Days are leaping before me like tadpoles
deluding my mind into the justice of heaven.
The hands of clocks tell of wicked brains
spidering in the stretching universe.
I wouldn't take long breaths again
to chase burnt butterflies
nor recreate them in my words.
I wouldn't believe the birds' wings
voted for cold enough cages
and gave in their sky to phantoms.
No, I wouldn't as I shouldn't.
Pensively I turned away
with my breath pent
holding space in my right eye
and laughing with my left one
at every mirror managing
to be a bridge over logic.

The End of the Fight

This head is a deferred night
surrounded by iridescent days
that pass like migratory birds
under the straying sunlight
This head brims with red wine
that looks like the blood of a lion
in the midst of battles.

This head, a Caesar on the shoulders
ordering my feet to wander
and enter the mouth of the unknown,
throwing me headlong in the bosom
of intense storms.

Dreams are rooted thoughts
in which nothing intervenes.
They act like demi-gods
invading space without machines.

This head is a frigate for sailors
who have been let down
by shy ships in lumpy oceans,
a victim of things hard to expound,
and a mourner of incomplete images
though it envisions the world
as a version of perfection
beyond the rubbles and damages.

Travel, and you won't finish the journey
of the infinite waters
Travel, oh stubborn mind in the sanctuary
of metaphors and wear the cloak of words.

This head feels heavy and left out
like a raven you don't much know about.
This head you hold between your hands
is a calm pasture contoured by ponds.
The future's phantoms are all grazing,
feasting upon the peril felt by every petal.

The eyes of life possessed with owning
everything forgetting a shroud has no pocket.
This head is a deferred night
surrounded by a kingdom of stars
shining like rare rubies with all their might
But only when they fall at the end of the fight
we'll understand we were lit by our own scars.

Life Treads Upon the Eyes of a Poet

Life descends from the axis of eternity
Like a rolling sun aflutter
after fogs are gone in their own vanity
fading away forever.

I am a window waiting for lethal light
and behind me my bewildered shadow
screaming and caught in the blue claws
of water that hold me tight with all their might.

I am trying to pull out my wet dreams,
my pictures from the valleys of oblivion.
I am brooding over the battle of beams
in their way to the far depths of Man.

I am climbing my rugged thoughts
easing the face of fear through the pen.
The future is under the feet of fierce beasts
with blood maps as their sole plan.

Life falls like a peculiar apple in the hands
of the haunted not far from doom.
Fate gnaws at the flesh it wants
and sees my shining bramble as a moon.

Life is an unknown wind cutting my fingers
with its deadly cold, throwing my face
into the past, into the mouth of rusty dust.

Life descends to make me run at last
after nothing. My shoes let me down,
slaying my ankles without mercy
while every hour rests there in its throne
like a princess whose aim is heresy.

Life treads upon the eyes of a poet
searching carefully his spacious heart
in the fertile ovule of a flower.

But after springtime, like a skilled tailor
it often weaves him a shroud made of mist.

Wandering Minds

To whom will you extend your hand, tree
if you are consumed by the flickering flames?
You are standing alone like the black
of a corpse between the mirror of water from
underneath and the hanging glass of heaven
above. To whom will you sway again so soon?

Who will wipe the ashes off your neck,
Oh tree, if it's not the feathers of fearful birds
roaming around the banes of their bleakness
like wandering minds burnt up
by the sweeping summer of illusion?

To whom will you bloom again, poetry
while words with a whole lot more to say
are floundering in a trap set by art's enemies
in their absolute selfishness?

They burn the arms of nature
and wrap language's weapons
in the shroud of a gesture.

To whom will we extend our hands
other than our own shadows which are
stumbling behind us and crushing our fires?

Blooming Heart

Life is a witch murmuring in my ears
devouring my blooming heart
on my ancestors' table
invaded by ants that settled on its scratches
to translate their ongoing anxiety.
Life is the neighing storms trapped
in our breath which pushes the sun upwards
the way Sisyphus reluctantly pushes his rock,
the way ants drag the fresh grains of wheat
and sugar without sweating or groaning.
The threads of light refuse to be gossamer
for me to wear at wreckage moments.
The marrow in my bones has ripened
and became as recondite as dynamite.
My frustrated feet are groggy with it.
I will explode words on the last blank page
of desire and excavate souls similar to anthills
created by seasoned mandibles.
On this ancient table I can hear the maelstrom
of history and the sounds of absent spoons.
I can hear dusty images calling my name.
They dance under my skin like flames.
Life is a witch murmuring in my ears,
devouring the blooming heart of a ponderer
sat at my ancestors' table.
Life is an invisible eye watching our footprints
fade far away behind bare bluffs and old ruins.

On the Platform of Loss

We are the progeny of light, cast into blackness.
We came from our distant absence
like lightning from the dream of God
on the grey pillows shaped by clouds.

Dust is our first great-grandfather
whose voice has been stolen by the wind
and whose sweat sponged by the sun
that slaughters stars and promises.

We became orphans in our motherlands,
strangers dragging us down and selling
us the reasons for our lives.
They sell us images of illusion on the platform of loss.

Everything got put out and in our eyes petrified
We only see werewolves eating their tails
and fighting tooth and nail out of greed,
plotting to invade the ships of hope floating in our hearts.

We are the progeny of the far beyond
but have been cast into the bottom
of an infinite to find ourselves on Earth,
this red rock accommodating all the contradictions,
this bluffing face harnessing
the tears of heaven and investing in a galaxy's
recondite remnants to make out of us
mere vociferations and machinations.

We compete forever and for nothing except
to break the awful isolation around existence.

Shadows

Palm fronds are the desert's
window to a deity's splendour.
The broad golden threads of light
separating these green leaves
stand like a black wolf's wounds
probing deep to the bone,
like the echo of a scream sneaking
between the teeth of a stoic comb
missing feminine pulchritude.
Now I understand why pigeons
lay their eggs under this shady ceiling,
eschewing the sun and its envy.
You'd rather imagine the ample openness
and dream of Heaven's vaults
from the tiny cracks in a dungeon.
You'd rather fathom light by degrees
and grow feelings before feathers.
Ascend like dust from earth upwards.
You'd rather be the dream shared by petals
on a rose to ride the teetering nightmares
sprouting from the infernal deep.
The eyes sometimes fly before the wings.
They carry with them the fractures of the soul
and take in their stride the burning weep.
Everything dead is again born here.
Yes, right here under the palm fronds
Even the grasses on this lonely rock
looks like blonde box braids
from the gentle shadows
swaying in tandem with the breeze.

Obsessions

In this corner of the vast world
poetry is born like a caterpillar
in the deep. It flutters to water
before the wind carries it to the reeds'
dry throats that form a choir against
the ugliness of autumn.
Throats know the meanings of words
way better than all dictionaries
because they turn them into glamour
and beauty on the bosom of space.
In this corner of the world
Poetry is born like a hearth fire,
like a red scream in the face
of the blind mischievous night.
The naivety of the world pursues
the singing on your chest, oh book,
and the music in your ribs, oh stubborn poet.
There are no eyes but this sparkling cinder,
this compass looking like a fallen
star clamped between my firm fingers.
No ears except the spicy breezes
taking hold of the soul like magnets.
Poetry is born from the shadow of a cloud
over men's heads, filled with obsessions
and veered into stunning destinations.

The Wings of Night

You are just a cloud, poetry!
Yes, a cloud that descends
on mysterious chests
vanishing in a crowd.
You don't have a clear shape
like the wound of the sun before it rises.
I find you ever-changing,
challenging as a sea grape.
You don't dedicate your heart
to one single word like me
nor give an appointment
to the window of imagination
as you fall all of a sudden
to distil your drink
from anything and from everything.
You are a storm messing
with the quiet of water,
with the blackness of ink,
with the eyelids of the bewildered.
You awaken the wings of a world
so sick of its eternal cage.
You are emotions and thoughts
as white and certain as death
on time's thirsty mouth.
You have no mirror except that
made of what is broken in us
and turned into invincible darkness.
Poetry, you only have a star in the sky
to light up for you night's wings
and melt away the cold bars.
You only have my wide awake eyes
where you'll explode more than one surprise.

The Face of the Moon

The face of the moon is the last thing
a pigeon sees on its own slaughter
by the dark while dancing with its wound
in the hands of death.
Blood oozing, covering the stem of a rose
like a red cloud resembling nothing,
dripping from the eye of a wolf irked
by distance and by the ice of despair.

The face of the moon is a puzzle of the dark
flickering between the past and the present
like a sacrifice above the worries of the wind,
a golden tear for the thirst of a dream,
a breast cut from Aphrodite's soul
and cast like a shrapnel to kill dogmas
in cold hearts and free magmas of the mind.

The face of the moon is the sun's innocence
of infancy after its disappearance behind time
and the recondite back of space.
We won't have the same shadows
and destinations here under the moon.
Our screams will be heard now.

The call of the waves will reach the ears of mountains
more clearly, and the hands of death
will be more merciful at the bottom
of this luminous chalice, hanging from
the invisible throne of God.

The last thing dust sees before it is imprisoned
in dew drops is the face of the moon,
before it weaves the long threads of absence.
How cruel and tormenting is absence.

The face of the moon: the last piece of cheese
a crow in vain opens its mouth for, and flies across.

The last thing a pigeon sees
on its own slaughter by the dark while dancing
with its wound in the hands of death
is of course the face of the moon.

Breath War

Now, darker grows in me the night.
It pushes by pain my pen to write.
Now, I hear breathing machines
moan like dissolving aspirins,
quiet is the night, and only coughs,
broken sounds, uncertain chests
where death's angel lovingly rests
to free the soul off handcuffs.

Now, you can't rhyme like me
when you feel that the world is a crime
you can't burn, either
as the tear I fight back becomes an ember.

Now, you can't weep like me,
I'm a desert of guilt and thirst for his words
yet all I find are eighty-one pages of silence,
sighs, souvenirs, and awful absence.
You, summer flower in the deep South,
you can't miss water
like his feverish mouth
housing death and turning paler.

In his departing eyes, a sea of messages
to the heavy blows of life's gale
a throat of petrified words
forsaken, cold like a winter grave,
There must be birds much bluer
than Bukowski's, in his heart;
birds that build their nests of hope
and demolish them every night.

No, you aren't here to understand
life's summary at the end.
Water he drinks from my hand
is a furrowing fire burning in me.

Death's beds around us
are of course undug tombs.
Tomorrow's bones: extra rooms
for new lives with a fuss.

The bed desires to take him
within a journey of long sleep -
I know it can't, for he's the memory
I will forever and ever keep.

The Soul's Rhapsody

Oh poetry, take me back to my father's shadow
while he reads fate on the face of clouds,
and fathoms life with his seasoned eyes,
while he smells petrichor approaching
fast like a healer for the ills in men
and in the air reminiscent of freedom.
Take me back to myself, to my soft pillow
under which I hide my new shoes
that I from time to time wake up to try.

Return me to me
the way my father's hand returns wheat
to the ground with the soul's rhapsody,
and broad sweeps
before at any moment rain hits us;
before hungry birds and ants devour
the seeds of creation inside my ribs.

Oh ink, carry me to my bare feet,
to the antique olive oil jar
which offers me a selfie, gives me back
my face, my hair, and my mouth's vapour
whenever I stare into it.

Carry me back, haemorrhage
to that leaking ceiling which imprisons
the invisible breasts of the azure
and squeezes the patience of stones.
Ah! I miss that small window above the door
where I used to hide cats eyes, I mean marbles.

I miss so much the view to trees from there.
I want to go up again on a barrel to that window
and drop in on the faithful traces of my hands.
Yes, my hands which groped for everything
precious I hid in there.

My hands hugging each other now as I sit
in the dark burning on my own with nostalgia.
No one burns with me except my cigarette.

Oh ink, no one would save me but you
Oh ink, take me to the vivid images of life,
keep me away, far away from 'the dead.'

Weight of Disappointment

Our neighbour used to raise pretty pigeons.
She would ask me to gather firewood,
Keep an eye on her sheep in those grassy green places,
and sometimes water her mule.
In return, she used to promise to give me pigeon eggs
or a pair of chicks to keep.

I would be on pins and needles until the sun appears
so that my parents allow me to go out and play.
But I would go to that hut where the birds live.
My eyes were ahead of me to see the white beaks
and the scintillating sea-blue feathers.

I was young and didn't realize
that such cunning is capable of making
a child search for his own heart
in childhood dream nests under those wings.
She knew how to separate my soul
from my hands and feet, from my entire body.

I used to do whatever she would ask me to do,
bring her water, run after her rooster,
catch it hold it in my arms as if I were a hero.
Perhaps she would prepare something
like couscous with chicken which I had to smell at a distance.

I remember myself running after it
and taking it out from under a prickly Aloe Vera.
She would promise me pigeon eggs
and little chicks without carrying out that promise afterwards.

I had done her all the favours.
My despairing eyes questioning one of her protruding teeth
about the thing for the sake of which my feet had to bleed.
That ugly tooth was like a knife to my neck.

I still feel it between my eyes
She would sarcastically, belittlingly reply:
"Don't you hear this voice?
Your mother is calling your name.
Run! Run now, and find out what
she wants you for."

I could feel tricks from gesticulations
and tones. As soon as I turned away,
she slammed her dusty door after me
as if she would never open it again.
In that moment drowning in despair,
I wished I could disappear
from any sort of masquerade.

If only my chest would become a similar hut
to accommodate all the birds of the world.
But unfortunately I left my heart there behind me
like a memory beating obstreperously
in the middle of those white eggs despite
the unbearable weight of disappointment.

The World Doesn't Care About Poetry

Why doesn't the world care about poetry
while all eyes are dripping with dark images
distilled from hearts that have been crushed
by hardships and sad nights?

Only a few carry the burden of this boring universe,
only a few turn tears
into a torrent of expressive words.

Why doesn't a poet appear on TV
and recite his poems to children
so that they understand that the night
is a door into distant imagination?

Why are poems not sold at the chemists'
like medicine and I would receive them
from a lady's eyes the colour of my dream?
Why won't you let the poetic flow take my fever
in its direction to the sanctuary of the soul?

This world has no listening ears
It just throws the bard into the dungeon
of oblivion where he might be seen
as a joke in the form of a phantom
who speaks the words of wizards and fools.

Why do you only see bodies in bodies
and disagree that poetry is the material
from which the air we breathe was created.

Where else aside from art could you find truth?
Where else would words live in peace?
This body containing me was only a heartbeat,
a fabric brimming with all that is recondite.

Sounds are the origin which builds
the tangible and solid things around us.
So, why don't you let poetry rebuild the rubble
you used to worship with verve?

Crescendo

This lofty palm tree is Earth's
green neck crowned with light.
Bunches of dates rise before the sun.
The bowing branches grateful to roots
create the shade of a rose window open
on the water's obstreperous depths.

Things spot their shadows
and magically illuminate them later.
Everything exists like bitterness
before it explores the inner sweetness
just like a palm tree standing as a bartender,
and blossoming with golden sapphires
after offering the wine in its thorny head
to the tapper on the top, holding his scythe.

There is more meaning to tap out and shed
with care in the huge tunnel of thoughts.
There are breathing pores and buried eyes
up there lovingly dripping with songs.
There is an entire ancestry immured inside,
way deep underneath this dry skin.
I am pretty cool with nature's indifference
to the short-sightedness of Man.

A third eye only fathoms the kernel of things;
A third eye pours out the conversations
I happen to have with prehistoric mornings.
This palm tree points to the blue diaphanous
forehead of time, to the echo of music
messing with fire's expanding waist as she dances on
and on until reaching her crescendo.

There is fire in palm wine
cause dates are edible embers dangling
from above thirstily for an unknown womb.
The rest underneath is ample ash
spreading and covering every part
except one fallen seed that dust carried
and blew up into millions of stars.
No dark would reach those benches
scintillating in the stoic azure,
No cruel hand could destroy the bridges
I built with words
No dream would stand out on my mind
without those eyelashes incubating palm wine.
My head is ramshackle like a ceiling devoid
of dreams, my body a flooded mine
by hail under lightning strikes
Here under this strange paradox
of fall and rise I come to be
and will disappear completely.

Nothing will remain of me but my eyes
as bullets for further battles with the dark.
Nothing with which I would dance
on the page with sounds except my fingers
that I didn't realize were originally dates
given by heaven to untie an oasis of emotions
from firm bonds and set it hence free.

The Space the Soul Sings

In the throes of worry you stay up
deprived, pensive, and wondering
how many a fellow you have considered
as your moon and stars
and whose embers you tightly hugged
so that he wouldn't get completely burnt,
how many times you sat meditating the scenes
of birds' breaking necks in the eyes of storms
but couldn't hold back your pent feelings!
In the throes of your prehensile depths
You never put your beloveds out.

Rather than distance, than coldness,
than silence, you just wanted to push the boat
out for the wedding of melody and moans.
How many breezes got trapped in a flower's thorns,
how many butterflies have turned
the speaking behind the backs into spots
shining bright they happily bragged about!

How many thundering bolts
you discovered on the faces of foes
and which bestowed on you words
you didn't know would be verses!
How many dreams you saved from
the obsidian mouth of the night!

How many miles you had to walk
within the ribs of this tremendous cosmos,
before inspiration smote your blood
like a magic wand searching a hiatus
in your throbbing veins.

How many times Muse appeared
and you chased it deep in your unknowns
as if the sky were there as the beat
of your untethered heart!

You grabbed the mural of your ego
the way an eagle snatches its prey
and flies above the anguished ships.
You rose higher with your own sky
because of the space the soul sings.

I Don't Know Where
I Lost my Mind

Life is so many folds and dark depths.
I don't know where I lost my mind
nor how to hold my thoughts
that became a compass for the wind.
My body is a galaxy far away from light,
swimming in the sphere of illusion
without a thinking mind.
My eyes are two bullets in memory,
my staring face, a battleground for legends.
I cut my teeth on the thorns of a rose
at the beginning of the road.
I fell headlong into peculiar echoes
rising from time
and danced like water at the bottom of a well.
The rain pierced my ears with its music.
Clouds were crying like squeezed sponges.
Now I can sing and dance to the sky.
May it inspire me with a mind
that doesn't perish when mixed with emotions.
I am down here, contoured by red walls
made of ancient rocks.
My right knee is in a mudslide
And my left one, lonely like a crow
unable of giving an explanation for his failure.
Life is a well, its mouth is staffed with clouds
but its bottom is my pathless chest
filled with the roots of bitter grapes.

Arrows of Metaphors

Many more green forests
are still growing in our minds
like beautiful poems.
Homeland is not firewood for your fire
as you may deem, you passer-by!
You are all deceivers hankering
after power, thinking that it is a mirror
of your own ambitions.
You blind minds! You see nothing but fire
as a rose in the middle of oceans of grass.
Homeland is not the wounds of birds
under clouds of smoke
Nor is it the essence of truth in collecting
votes inside ballot boxes.
Selfishness is building an illusion
in your heads and adjusting it to your whims.
Selfishness turns people into wolves
on the tops of mountains to burn the sky.
You are all mercenaries who won't live long.
The country is mangled in the arms
of the unknown and the fangs of greed.
Many clouds will still rise from human hearts
and will be raining traps.
You are all convoys towards the void.
A whole people behind you is breathless
carrying a desert of despair in his eyes.
We are darting the arrows of metaphors
at your lies and uprooting fire
from the liver of burning hills.
We still see bees as our unique voice
in those ballot boxes
cause we crave life and sweetness
like most children.

Fire and Water

Fire and water are two bodies
having the same shadow.
They dance the same dance to the wind
and share our dreamy eyes.
Fire is a rose in the dark
that I smell with my dead fingers,
that I draw in my blunt memory
and from time to time I upturn the embers.
Water tells me about the freedom of the air
on mountain tops
and searches a way to the roots of absence.
It turns into flowers of all the colours,
cures the cracks and wounds in earth.
Water and fire are the same
because they absorb each other
in their search for an identity and a name.
The one speaks of the other
and steals the other.
Water and fire are thieves
crossing the night and hiding everywhere.
They sleep to the laughter of children
and rise to the sound of existence.
Water and fire are two strangers
who don't know how to go back home,
two astray visitors looking into the mirror
of absurdity like two 'I's in one poem.

The Thorns of Time

I got away from everything,
wrapped myself in my shadow.
Together we crossed the tunnel of sadness.
How lonely life is without shadows
that would make of you two!
How long the way to humanity is!
I'm still wandering like a galaxy swimming
in an infinite space.
Grey thoughts run through my mind
to explode with the rising of each new sun.
I took my shocks and worries with me
so I wouldn't forget.
I left everything behind
and journeyed with my burnt out heart.
I even left my laughter and my mouth
which is in love with its pangs of regret.
I walked away from my body and left it
drown alone in cold water
and savour the salinity of disappointment
there. I got away from everything
I wrapped myself in my shadow
and we crossed like twins the tunnel
of life and the stabbing thorns of time.

Life is a Movie

Politicians are actors, after all.
The stage is dotted with thorns and deprived of thoughts.
Good Actors, yes!
But we don't need actors who complicate things.
We don't need actors
whose eyes are meant to be explosives
in the short and long run.
We are born to take roles for life itself is a movie.
However, all the roles are dirty, you know
and Man is always berated for not interpreting
the happenings around right.
We need masks to judge things right.
We lack blinders to get illuminated by.
One is mistaken without a mask instead of a face.
A politician should be good at tragicomedy.
He is this permanent, god-smacking
mixture necessary for progress.

All the roles require an illusory amalgam.
When they accuse you of wearing masks,
that is the moment they start playing their role.
It's all a game, a world much like Golding's Lord of the Flies,
inner beasts on everyone else's behalf,
worn out minds trapped and clogged like toilet bowls.
So they amalgamate everything as such,
they blend religion and politics and then try to separate them.
But we never witnessed them doing this nor that.

In reality, they do nothing save that they dilute
the poisons of deception into the limitless void.
They link up the scattered bits of hybrid scenarios.
They fritter away time and startle the future.

But for God's sake, whose children
are poverty, unemployment, and the miserable conditions?
Are they the children of religion? Of politics?
Or of this invisible, non-materializable mixture?
Why do governments create enemies by fabricating concepts?
What is the difference between political Islam
and Islamic politics?

Why don't they add sunlight and the sound
of the wind to their speeches and statutes?
Why do leaders delay our lives and cast them
far away in the distant unknown?
What is this war in the minds for,
a war that eats everything before it is ripe?
It's an unnecessary war fuelled by mutual fears.
Half of politics is this unknown in which we are steeped;
the other half is when absurdity is spoken and written.
It's absolute absurdity, for religion is olive oil,
and nothing mixes with it.
Politics is the specks of sand at the bottom of a streak,
economy is abysmally down and we know it's a truth,
a bitter truth.

They rush religion into the realm of metaphysics
and clothe politics with a bastard philosophy.
They cry over the homeland before strangers
and flee to the point of tampering with abstract concepts.
The musicality of language, if ever there were any,
Won't pull the masses and the lower dregs of society
out of the gutters.
Democracy means nothing, and dictatorship
is a cloud made of the vapours that our mouths
send as an expression of both despair and frazzledness.

Distance has Drunk My Life

The villages are scattered over the hills and plains,
linked together by narrow paths and lanes.
Every day I cross these distances,
I fill my eyes with the mirrors of water
emanating from the ground and breathe the colors
and scent of wormwood mixed with thyme
that dense forests resembling green waves of grass exude.
As a small child I used to enjoy the wind whipping my face.

My eyes shed tears from the cold air.
My schoolbag on my back
was full of books, notebooks and other things.
My mother would put bread, salted olives, and butter
for me and wrap them in a plastic bag so my possessions
wouldn't get dirtied.
I carried death and agony on my little knees.
Words were gathering like migratory birds in my chest,
like the bullets I fired on the exam paper
as I had to describe what I had witnessed on a rainy day.
I see my teacher scratching her forehead
with her fingernails as she was reading my paper.

She would look into my eyes, or in other words,
into my infinite depths.
I can still feel my feet stained with mud
I can still hear my father's voice calling and shaking my body.
Today I am only half myself;
my other half is words not born yet,
a storm of dreams stuck in spider webs.
I still remember the textures of the distant past,
the face of my grandmother, and her hypnotizing songs
filled with the gasps of patience.
A grape tree grew in the place where she used to sit

beneath the Tamarisk tree.
Grapes are the colour of her dry mouth from loneliness.
A pigeon incubated its eggs successfully
in the barrel where she used to hide
firewood for the merciless ice of winter.
The villages have not changed much.

I see an ember in each palm I shake hands with.
I am surprised by the sharp arrows darted from all directions.
The walls of the old houses were cracked
by the dark's fingers that split rocks in halves.
Mother's fingers are still visiting my hair
burdened with dust, grazing in it like the oxen
which lost their destination.
The villages are sad, the wind is whimpering
over the misery of the place.
The wicked sleep in the ovary of the rose
and change into perfume.

They haunt the neighbourhoods like zombies
and slaughter love with the fangs of death.
They rail at every cloud like the children of fire.
The house is sad and the distance has drunk my life.
It turned me into a thread of heres and nows.
Where do I stand exactly now in this vast universe ?
Am I a scream in the wind?
The place is a dumb mother, a seasoned artist in Nature.
I will defeat the miles and travel
endless roads like the echo of a bullet.
I will count on my firm feet only.

Tobacco Factory

Give me in exchange for the air
you covered with your dancing clouds
packs of little high-giving sticks
to help this bitter time vaporize.
You took my share of air
and sold me to unwelcome sneezing
and burning, itching around the eyes.
I want the new constitution to guarantee
this 'strange' right to me.
Cigarettes are free as almond roses up there
but my chest is imprisoned in illusion
like firewood wishing to be shrouded in fumes.
I want to smoke and nurture a good health
in poetry.
Do you understand, Tobacco Factory?
I need a wider space in my head
to plant luminous cinders far ahead
and ease the trespassing of injustice.
You took more space than anyone else,
Tobacco Factory.
Yes, you took more room on land, in space
and became like a destiny.
My coffee is lonely, Factory!
It's kind of unbearable bitter
cause they buried sugar in the graves of bees
and like wolves sympathized with the plebia.
My mouth is bitter, and this damned
summer is again bitter.
I only have the sweetness of cigarettes
left to offer as red eyes for the blind night.
So please Factory, don't rob me of this delight.
Don't be a phantom among us bequeathing
white tails skyward to already departed souls.

A Hell with Wings

The horizon is a piece of black cloth.
My heart, a night for cockroaches
crying it out, a land without water,
a glowing, roaring air
which drains dry my eyes
fleeing to a cloud in my head
and feeding on the far light behind.
It's a hell with wings
passing through the silent windows
and devouring my bewildered face.

The Last Chance

Why don't we distribute sugar
among ants and bees?
The ants will sculpt for us flutes
From reeds to play the long distances
with, and break down barriers.
The bees will yield sweet tea
very much like honey,
tea that we will share in an oasis of tranquility
and must be happy with.

Why don't we try drinking bitter coffee
and eat at the same time cactus roses,
and pomegranate buds with our eyes
until we tell no more of hunger.
Isn't this possible particularly
as the reason behind life colours our eyes?
Isn't it possible when an entire people
just knows what they want.

Why don't we delude children
into thinking the desert is a piece of cheese
melted in the mouth of a fox
and which will return only in the form
of wheat ears that they'd give to a sad crow.

Why don't we convince flowers
they are kisses for the dead
that shouldn't be picked,
that graves are bee boxes
seeking peace and fresh water?

Why didn't we learn that we are
on the verge of danger
as we enter a stage
that only welcomes masks,
or else our feet will sink deeply
into the tarmac of drama.

Why do we distribute brains
among gargoyles and have bodies
think with the tails of scorpions
to defend themselves against the Haves' canes
Why does one still sing his burnt out soul
while the last chance has vanished like a foal
in an absolute mirror of dust.

This Air is Strange

This air is the cry of a prisoner
behind walls as cold as oblivion,
steadfast as the eyes of children
after the victory of darkness
and the disappearance of roads.

This air is mist in disguise
a sponge for songs, for the feathers of mystery
in the dancing of trees to wagons of clouds.
These trees and their shades breathe like me.
This air exudes petrichor, exhumes phantoms.
This air is omnipresently strange.

The stone under which I hid my first cigarette
breathes like me, records the murmurings
of escaping abstruse waters.
This air taunts the stoic, obsidian ashes
on an unseen stage.
This air is strange.

It wrecks the stars on sea waves.
This air is the sigh of water,
the jerk of fish outside nets,
the kiss given by a rose to the palm
of its picker, despite its bleeding wound.

This air is strange:
We see it because we don't know it.
God hates to colour thoughts;
He loves invisible mirrors and deep reflections.

This air is a prayer without wings,
a new being struggling to born.
This is air is the thief of life
deceiving us through void's mask.

This air is unbreakable glass
and dissolved blasphemy in a divine mirror,
the picture of place and time as one entity.
This air handles piles of suffocation with care,
frees the petals of spring and the pangs of worry.

This air is where we register rage
and out-yell time eternally.
This air is God's only heir.
This air is omnipotently strange.

No Matter How Deep You Can Dive

Night arrives home.
The moon sits on rooftops,
waiting for the birds to fall asleep
to charge them with dreams
and dry their frozen tears.
She gathers the prayers of the broken,
prayers stuck in the windows
like blazing fires to carry on its back
towards the clouds.
The whole world dies.
Brimming heads with worries
drown in pillows like tired sailors
in the magnetizing view of waves.
Time wears a different cloak,
Dawn's first ember shows up
and real drama hides behind light.
The sun studying a country
which embraces despair in its arms,
which drinks from the salty sea water
until twelve million couples of lips whiten.
A ship's plank savouring its own wounds
and floating on long decades of absence.
Whole sale of future dreams,
privatization of knowledge, of air, of Art.
Banks of promises on the brink of lies.
Light is the brother of fog,
the back of the night from the other side.
The same old songs, the same faces
giving themselves a black eye.
The neck of patience is sky-high.

Frustrated feet about to sprout
in their place like spiny plants
ready to prick pigeons
and pluck their feathers.
The sun is blind and always careless.
It didn't light up a corner for rhythms
and images in poetry houses
and never warmed a cold coffee
or icy emotions near a fireplace.
It only looks for tears to drink,
then turns its back like a thirsty jar.
What is more, it covers up for crooks
and chooses blindness by its own glare.
I turn all tears into words and metaphors
as soon as they start to form.
The more I rhyme, the cooler the storm
in my implacable, seething eyes.
The sun laughs at my depictions of it
in my verses and sponges their meanings.
It never takes a different road
or rids humanity of a much heavier load,
never takes my quill to scrape the sky
with but it ignores that my heart can fly
and that my words are feathers
a poem wears and turns away.
The sun is an eyewitness
that doesn't speak the truth
but covers up for all the crooks.
Under it, there are human wolves
mistaking hearts' limpidity for hen houses.

A whole Mafia muffling the future
and fashioning a rosy picture.
The mood strikes anarchy and monopoly.
The drink of marmites is cooking oil.
Hungry masses begin to boil.
The sun, an absent-minded historian,
a Tabula Rasa refusing to learn.
The only mission taken for granted
is just to peep and blindly burn.
Dreams escape from prisons
like existential questions and smiles
on the faces of mothers and fathers.
You won't understand anything
as long as you are alive.
No, you won't understand
no matter how deep you can dive.
The sun is a mirror that absorbs.
It doesn't reflect.
It's not like water; it has no voice,
makes no sounds, and gives nothing back.
It's not like the wind; it doesn't bother the trees.
It's not like a mine as it hasn't exploded yet,
or revealed the enigmas it buries inside.

Thirst Day

Today, clouds visit our sky
They form from eyes we don't see.
Trees are moving towards a deep dream
to live rain before its falling.
Birds do not want their songs to be heard
out of respect for the envisioned rain showers.
Today, cigarettes have a different taste
and coffee is as warm as a sea of black eyes
that spare lightning.

The wind is freed from Hell's oubliettes
and has buried the sun under water
to ask hovering swallows for a dance show
in the awesome vastness yonder.
Today is Thirst Day for drowning in time;
a day for halting spinning clocks,
tying hours' feet to rooms' rafters
until real winter misses my rhyme
and starts on my door knocking.

The Dead Inside

The country is doubled up in pain.
Everyone wants to leave.
The sun sponged the shade
and condemned the sea.
Water is worried about its fate
in lanes it knows nothing of.
The cat's dream has run away
for beggars expelled them
from the paradise of trash.

Despair is warming up to a fire
pictured by a rippling mirage.
We drink the wind like gargoyles
and dream of ships full of beauties
and churning casks for oblivion
and for warding off our blues.
We need to chase the depression
sitting on a streetlight pole
like an invincible owl.

Everyone rushes the train of time.
Maybe tomorrow will bring sunshine.
But life is too short and days are shorter.
Hearts are toughening and no longer lithe.
Life's a wink and days are the tails of black cats,
the green flies, and the echoes of larks.
We wear smiles lest we go insane.

We don't care too much about clothes.
We wear smiles that we learnt
from the mouths of the dead
and from the red autumn leaves
aspiring to lovely heavens.

But my mother didn't teach me
how to put on a fake smile
and face with it this cruel world,
a galloping void towards a stage
full of calculating, cold masks.

Our lips are little graves yielding
patience, and hiding behind them
sharp bones that in nightmares
crush one another with rage.

Our lips sipped an ocean of coffee
without having our thirst doused
as if the dead inside us drank everything.

Mere Imaginings

Humanity has not arrived yet
Noah's Ark is still at sea.
Ugly hands blocking the butterflies' way
My eyes boarding a pack of cigarettes.
Fools forget that I am ready to play with death
as children used to do when they wrap owls
in newspaper sheets and set to them fire
To make the first warplanes.
Those burnt wings rise higher and higher
like small red windows opening on hell.
At least they fly despite the flames.
But your old passport is now an owl
in depth of darkness, and a fox is sniffing it,
grinning and feasting upon your frittered time.
He hides it from you and you have to come back tomorrow.
Two whole weeks like this.
Humanity is a bad check, a deer in a drawing
on the back of dust surrounded by wild dogs,
cold bones wearing flesh, flesh wearing cloth.
Noah's Ark is still at sea.
Everyone are shaving their beards under the current
to look sheen and dazzle whales.
The moon is a breast milked by myths,
the sun a butterfly without wings,
driven by the wind,
and rolling down the necks of mountains.
Human heads are just a demons' sanctuary.
Humanity has not begun to be.
We are just a joint point in a long process,
we are mere imaginings in gentle skulls.
Our dream is a good whining in wine shops
and a sighing like winds upon these stones.

The Green-Tattoo Hand

While I am stirring my third coffee
a green-tattoo hand overlooks my book
and stretches to my phone stealthily.
A green hand the colour of my country,
the odour of hunger, the shape of a hook
fails to fish the aid of memory.
It must be hunger behind every sad look.
No need to say sorry, green hand!
or lose face cause I do understand
it's all a matter of hook and crook.
Listen hand, try not to rob, just try
for the more you sweat, the luckier you get.
Try, and if you fail, be a little Robin Hood.
Either way you are in a greener oubliette.

Images Beyond the Page

I don't know if it's the morning's face
carrying a progeny of beginnings
or the back of the sun rising in haste,
blazing with men's weary toiling
in the closing chasms of rage
like buried images beyond a page.
I don't know if time accumulates fate
in light and changes it into dark
that I should more than contemplate,
wash well with the dew of dawn,
and hang beside other garments lain
on the clothesline.
One day we wear this dark on the way to God
through the hammering ribs of a deep grave.
We'll leave the sunlight lagging behind
and tricking existence like a cruel knave.
I don't know if children consider the sun
as a nightmare because they see its teeth
with which it bites and smashes corn
and electrifies mirage from underneath
as if it were water without weight,
water banned from the sea as a detainee.

I Want

I want a glass containing the sea
and a desert never tiring of making
sandy breasts for the mouths of strangers
after their fights with the sterile fingers of lightning.
I want a rose without petals to bedeck
with a crown made of the Dead's shroud cloth,
so that they can see the hell of life through
for a while and then fall back anew
to sleep like old books read by dust
under the seething light of stillness.
I want a glass to be filled to the rim
by a bartenderess whose neck knows nothing
of the fangs of ice.
I want her heart that bleeds with wine, rushing
the blooming of songs before my eyes.
I'd harvest her pain with my drunken hands.
I want a bottle of bitterness, a boat, a book
and a couple of scythes to reap the waves,
so that they do not conceal her look
from me, so that I can see her, always.

Effulgent Waterfalls

At every peeping dawn
I cast my dry fingers
as wood to a rose's fire.
I offer them to the dark
searching death's attire.
The night is a desert
and my hands are tents
for the here-and-now.
I do not master anything
except the writing of noise
on the deaf ears of ire.

The exploding cries of stars
feel like eggs in larks' nests
that one day will return to God
the way nightmares do to skulls
when sunlight abruptly besieges
and absorbs their cold poison.

These barkings are lyrical songs
for ghosts and unknown traces
after the emigration of sleepers
towards their own eyes.

This night is a lifted pond
for the thirsty wounds of wolves,
spreading like ashy clouds
to steal the gold of the sun
and hide it deep down
in the frazzled, forlorn chasms
in the womb of time.

I break my dry fingers
as the only wood
and food for contemplation
and pick the hours and days,
and the threads to my destination
with both my teeth and fingernails.

I will arrive and cook my morning
coffee on my blazing palms
with images of want for bleeding
and washing over croaking qualms.
I will arrive at a better understanding
of time's effulgent waterfalls.

The Moon Rises from Your Hair

It's midnight and tiny stars start
to bud on your dimpled face
subduing the night with grace.
As I take your hand and we walk
the moon rises from your hair
like a lantern at the core of dark.

Our rippling laughs in the air
finish off the work of dreams.
We venture into each other's unknowns
charged with passion, so unaware.
My hand stealthy frolics and drowns
like a wanderer in your gypsy hair.

It's midnight and the arc
of love bends, quick over us.
Our talk in the form of whispers
half-platonic, half-romantic.
You heave sighs almost volcanic
reeking with vodka, non-static.
The moon revels in your moans
and bows to your breasts.

I harvest the future's distant tones
and ruin demons' hulking attic.
The neck of darkness stretches in vain
Love fills the heart and washes over my brain.
The moon sleeps on your face,
wherever I hide it spots my place.

I wait for you with ample arms
and my blood arousing lusty storms.

I water the roses on your lips,
for there is a well inside my ribs
where my heart stays and thinks.
I am in love at first glimpse
I find your fingers a round of drinks
shining bright and giving winks.

The moon rises from your hair
in a mellifluous, flickering twerk
unusually feeling debonair
and melting with the song of a lark.

I Contemplate My Eyes

A word is a pigeon perching
on the back of a paper.
Meaning, a feather that hasn't yet appeared.
I do not know if words fly from books
and return to minds
and then again go back without being seen.
Perhaps the letters are just shadows
of what we think or feel.
I am good at rhyming on my pillow
when I drop dead in deep sleep.
I compose dreams and forget them
and at dawn I contemplate my eyes
on the wall mirror
and write on the images of butterflies
lured by the mad roses of the fields.
A word is a city under the rubble,
a kitten digging it up for the sake of warmth.
Meaning is that warmth
in the bottom of a bottle.
I don't know if I die at every word
I write or if I am born again.
When I write, I can't breathe.
I rather see my poem turn into a long breath
like a running river while I am an ember
hoping to dissolve in the stream of water.
Meaning is an awaited messenger,
a murmuring echo from a dumb mouth.
A word is a resting prayer on white paper.

I Just Want Nothing

I want nothing
except an ocean of sweet grapes
that a white girl squeezes
with her lightning-like teeth
and turns into wine in her breasts.
Milk will be my coffin when I grow old.
I just want to place my head on a pillow
of a princess who never knew love
and then sleep like a cat after all the bars
had closed before him.
I want to draw the fish in a girl's head,
Know the shape of her hands,
the hymns her soul sings while she is in bed.
I want nothing
but the female of the clouds to shower me
and turn my right arm into a river,
and my left one into a green road.
I wish to be a homeland to the whole world,
a sea of absence and a desert for aching
in silence and for crying it out to dunes.
I just want to have the speed of deer
to keep abreast with galloping mountains
leading to galaxies,
to tread upon my eyes with my dry heart,
scrape my nose against a poem on love
and heave sighs of peerless romance.
I want nothing
I just want nothing.

Days are Wolves

You keep whisking us away in stunning vistas
We hear sounds tearing apart the silent night
At times a beast sprouts out from the closest part
Fear catches the eye and many a star darkens
Each new day makes you number one in troubles
Each new day rises bitter bile in throat then flies!
It waits somewhere in space till Man is buried.
Days, you keep rolling us down endless roads,
And you crush dreams like as if they were toads.
We show bigger like suns and moons in their rising
But you dusk on us and death starts the hunting...

The Beginning of All the Colours

Ash is the beginning of all the colors.
It sleeps for eons in the eyelids of the sun
to finally give birth to fire in a dream.
Stars are the night's active bacteria,
the loyalty of roses to the rain,
and the encrypted messages to darkness.
Dawn is a red-blood beach to drown
minds in the hustle and bustle of life.
Ash is a cigarette's journey to the unknown
for your sake and a bottle's cataclysmic dance
after emptying their venom like glass vipers
into burnt out hearts after long wanderings.
Windows are blue daffodils growing in walls
and a blazing summer's blind thirst.
What's more? The grasses on muddy roofs
are goats' dreams in the years of drought.
They are green ashes and delayed fires.
Rain is but bars to trap in dust after storms
and give it some thoughts.
Death is a half-cry sending you in a tailspin,
a widespread lie that a volcano can't believe,
causing ash is the beginning of all the colours.

No Meaning in Hesitant Words

No peace other than the peace of mind.
No riches, no ecstasy bought with money.
The truest love requires cuddling
for which the lovers go blind.
No fresh air as that on the peaks
of mountains, no wings will fly high
and in-between them an ill heart.
No pulchritude matches yours, no darts
no swords pierce this dark like your eyes.
No sweetness outside those little dimples
in your cheeks resembling the reddest red
in roses dancing in wheat fields.
No peace other than the love we trust.
No paradise, no loveliness, no meaning in hesitant words.
Our love will be the dulcet throat for all birds,
the torrential rain from the udders of clouds.
No peace other than the talk of our hearts,
No rest, no dreams, no future outside romance.

Wilting Arms Reaching for Hugs

I wish I could catch the wind's hair
and tie it to the trunk of a palm tree
the way I tie a mare.
The wind blew my wandering mind
reflected in beer mugs.
I am wilting arms reaching for hugs.
Deep dreams flooded my mouth
with a bitterness that bugs.
I wish I could catch the wind's hair
and bestow it to my beloved
so that the smile I crave flashes
somewhere above to give me a ride,
so that our hearts will be out
of bodies' cages like two prayers so devout.

Churning Minds

If you are a stranger
ask the mountains about the way
to the face of the sky,
ask the sea wave about the trails of ships
reeking of absence.
If you are a stranger
cast you hand like a question
on the chest of darkness,
make your cigarette your sixth finger
reddening before your own eyes,
ask it about your face hovering
above imagination and under water,
ask the rose about the source
of its colour and fragrance.

Ask these heads about the sudden
invasions of grey hair.
If you are a stranger
just get armed with the presence of bees
at waterways.

Sail with your attracted heart to water.
Arm yourself with the worlds in words,
with the mud balls encompassing homelands.
Ask this ceiling about the blackness of the night
and fill your ribs with the storms of the impossible.

If you are a stranger
slaughter words one after the other on blank pages.

Let it be borne in your mind that ink
is a reflection of your imprisoned blood,
the inflection of your eternal presence

you have been searching
outside in a transient world,
a presence running like hour hands
and drawing rippling circles of meaning.

Ask time about time.

Ask these mothers' eyelashes about
their defeat of distance.

Ask their wrinkles about the destination of tears' rivulets.

Ask the bewildered and hapless
about their churning minds
counting down the minutes
until they turn into empty crocks.

The Torches of Art

Where will birds' throats and songs fade
When the sun gets suffocated
and becomes a ball of blackness
neither the neighing oceans
nor the squelching ghosts
ahead would be able to awaken
from its abysmal drowning?

How could I write my heart
and read it out to twilight
while these eyes are home
for angst and absence?

Which direction will dreams
go and who will absorb the foam
of anger and respond to the soil's
aspiration and roaring hunger
when the sun like a round-shaped
loaf of bread falls into a deep hole
dug by the hidden egos behind time
and is shared among strange systems.

No more of the chains of hours
and days and years.

The same old discourse
of shivering wind. It's just one boat
vacillating without direction.
No action while it's all destruction.

The same taste of disappointment
since a BMW government.

The eye of patience watching the future.
Maybe a bull from the nowhere
ploughs this dark pitching flickering
light by his horns in the arms of the masses
after this sun like a big bakery of hope
splinters, freezes and finally locks.

No windows on the memory of light
No vision or decision, no weapons
left in this maelstrom except the torches of art.

A Scream from Her Eyes

A scream from her eyes
Ignites my dry fingers.
I write the ache of fire
in her shrimp shadow.
A scream loud enough
to rip off the hearts of wolves.
It crosses the leaden skies
as if it has been suppressed
for so many centuries.
This beauty explodes
In front of my freezing body
from the roaring cold wind
and the salt of distance
that wiped out half
of the flowers I have been
watering with reassurance.
A woman as avid as waves
to cling to the top
of a nearby mountain,
as ready for anything
as the blood in my veins,
Knocking on my lips
with her whispers.
Her tears are sown
in broad sweeps
like the seeds of love
in my mind and soul.
Snow sold winter its dreams
surrendering to her hair and arms.
A distant silver star
on the forehead of dawn
illuminates this envious dark night.

These rooms have increased
in size as if to receive
the torrential emotions.
These windows suddenly turned
into blue cameras to photograph
a couple of ripe doves
sleeping on her chest.
A second striking scream
as she steps in the room
breaks out like the hiss
of a morning train
that stops at no station,
that knows no destination
The door closed behind us.
I devoured the snow stuck
on her arms and we feasted
upon the defeat of winter, laughing
and burning like two engines
under test. Night felt left out
and all the wolves fell silent.
My words drowned in the pond
of her maddening images
and we collided into
each other like two magma floes
from separate volcanoes.
I don't remember anything
in that healing heat except
me asking or maybe imploring:
"Don't knock on my heart again.
Let it languish in its own cell."

Passers-by

We walked long on the road and fell
we stood tall and no towel did we throw
though wounded by a word's scalpel
We left distance behind burning and aglow
We had for guide the eyes of patience,
and with our hands we strangled the evil crow.
A dancing desert inside our heads
welcomes the shadows that suddenly show
Solace were the people we came to know
But from evil ones we have tasted woe.
Time drained our hearts dray
and lectured beauties to the hapless eye.
Life has tight belts we had to fray
as we fade away like passers-by

Demise Behind the Eyes

Oh sea, no doubt you were a butterfly wing
swept away by the torrent and
had its blue colour melted in God's light.
No doubt you were the weep of the absent
and their demise behind the eyes.
Perhaps a part of me in you is what made waves
break and fall on each other like drunkards.
The relentless burning sand has absorbed
the sounds of shrieking ships and dried
the blood from each bleeding vein.
You were a butterfly seduced by the sky's eternity
but was brought back by the autumn rain
to Earth's blunt memory.
Excuse me, sea.
You were what you were.
You were the sweat of dreamers seeking quiet
in a turbulent tunnel all disquiet.
Oh sea you are small, so small
like a shard from a mirror on which love
has convinced an Innamorato of the beauty in pain.
You were a rolling dew drop, sea
on a pondering petal before jutting thorns
to scrape and puncture it playfully.
You were the only road the heart takes
to reach the mind,
You were a butterfly wing in the eyelids
of wrong time.

Behind the Dark

Oh death, do not be late!
I brought you a book, and a devil's skull
which I picked with my pickaxe.
Take me now, I've done my job behind the dark.
My grave will be here
on this huge round table called Earth,
this table where the wind fights the roots of a dream,
Where the moon has entrusted its blood to the sea.
Let me finish my cigarette first,
then take us together, death.
I'll leave you the coolest bottle
before I get too drunk.
Listen death!
I brought you my last breath
and closed my eyelids on the ugliness of the sun.
Take the blue distance between me and the sky
once my burial is done with.
Take everything if you want,
but please cover winter's back with my lonely coat.
Oh death, don't be late!
My feet are two raving reeds
dancing to storms that never abate.

Rough Roads

About Wheelsong Books

Wheelsong Books is an independent poetry publishing
company based in the ocean city of Plymouth,
on the beautiful Southwest coast of England.
Established by poet Steve Wheeler in 2019,
the company aims to promote previously unheard voices
and encourage new talent in poetry. Wheelsong is also
the home of the Absolutely Poetry anthology series,
featuring previously unpublished and emerging poets
from around the globe.

Wheelsong has more poetry publications in the pipeline!
You can read more about Wheelsong Books and its growing
stable of exciting new and emerging poets on the
Wheelsong Books website at: wheelsong.co.uk

Wheelsong publication list

- Ellipsis (2020) by Steve Wheeler
- Inspirations (2020) by Kenneth Wheeler
- Sacred (2020) by Steve Wheeler
- Living by Faith (2020) by Kenneth Wheeler
- Urban Voices (2020) by Steve Wheeler
- Small Lights Burning (2021) by Steve Wheeler
- My Little Eye (2021) by Steve Wheeler
- Ascent (2021) by Steve Wheeler
- Dance of the Metaphors (2021) by Rafik Romdhani
- Into the Grey (2021) by Brandon Adam Haven
- RITE (2021) by Steve Wheeler
- Absolutely Poetry Anthology 1 (2021) by various
- Absolutely Poetry Anthology 2 (2022) by various
- War Child (2022) by Steve Wheeler
- Hoyden's Trove (2022) by Jane Newberry
- Shocks and Stares (2022) by Steve Wheeler
- Autumn Shedding (2022) by Christian Ryan Pike
- Cobalt Skies (2022) by Charlene Phare
- Wheelsong Poetry Anthology 1 (2022) by various
- Rough Roads (2022) by Rafik Romdhani

All titles are available for purchase in paperback, and Kindle editions and some in hardcover on Amazon.com or direct from the publisher at: wheelsong.co.uk

Printed in Great Britain
by Amazon